SNAKE

COLORING BOOK

25 Large Intricate Snake-Themed Designs For Adult Relaxation And Stress Relief

THIS COLORING BOOK BELONGS TO:

TEST YOUR COLORS HERE

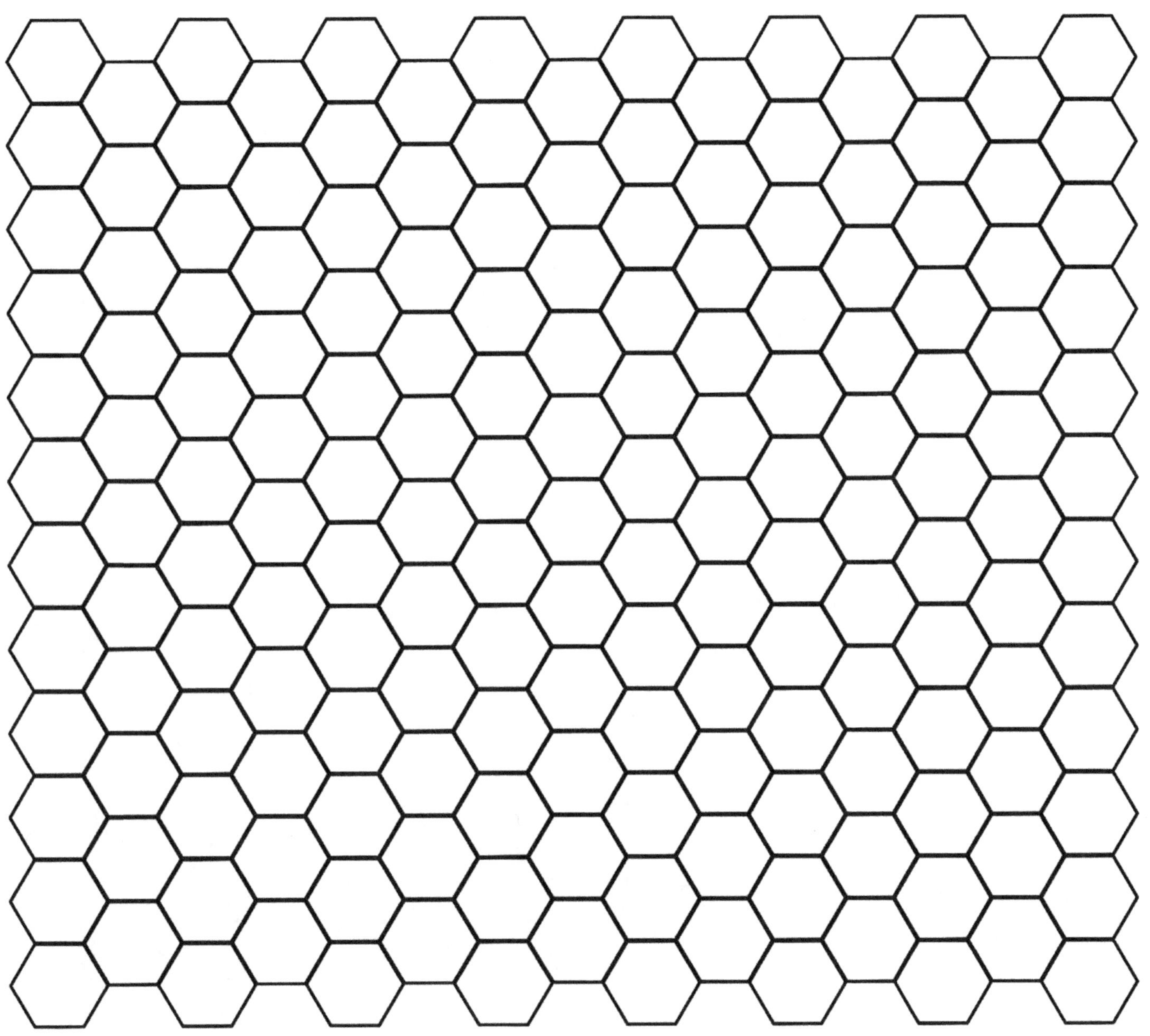

Using Markers? Minimize bleed-through by placing a
sheet of paper behind each page while you color

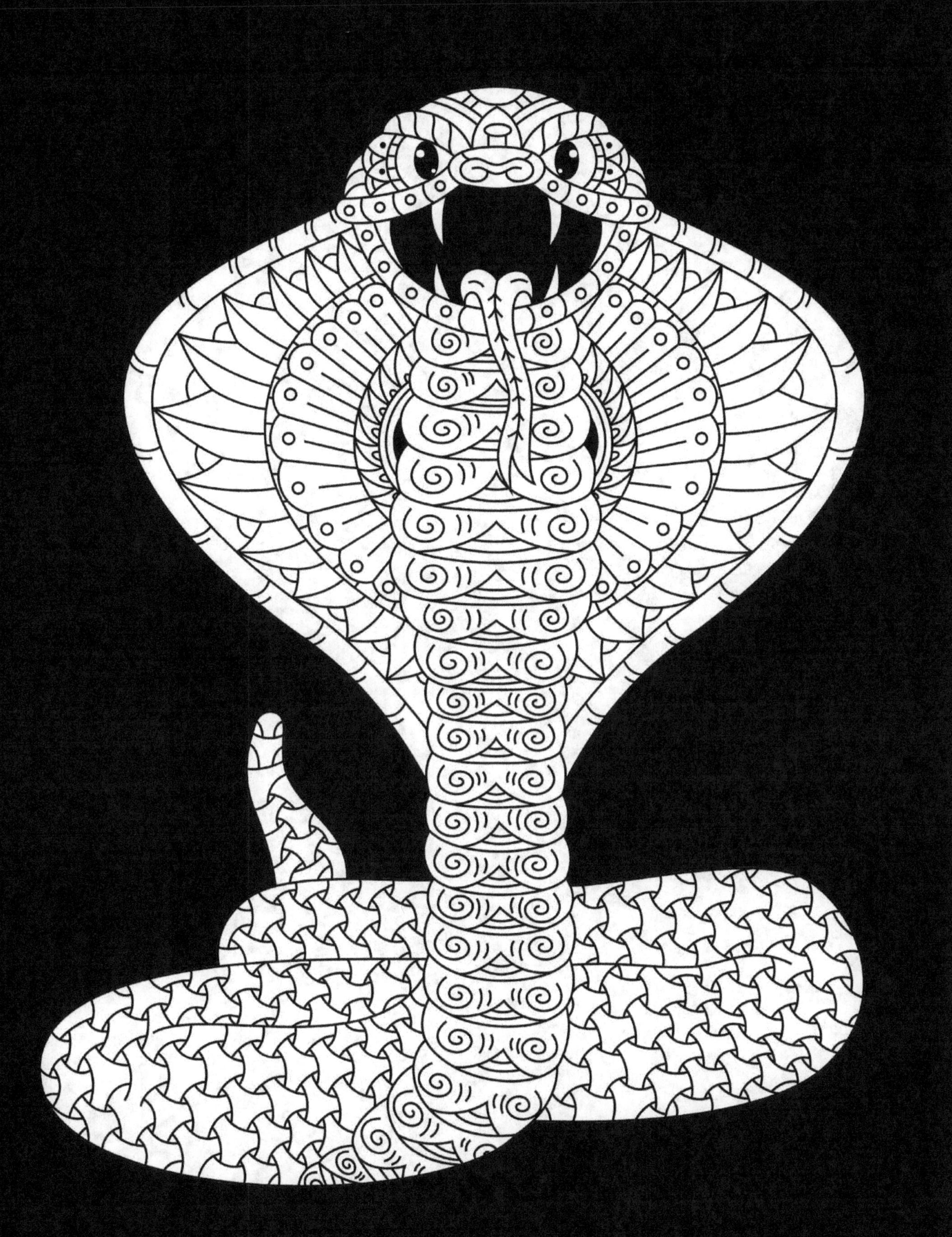

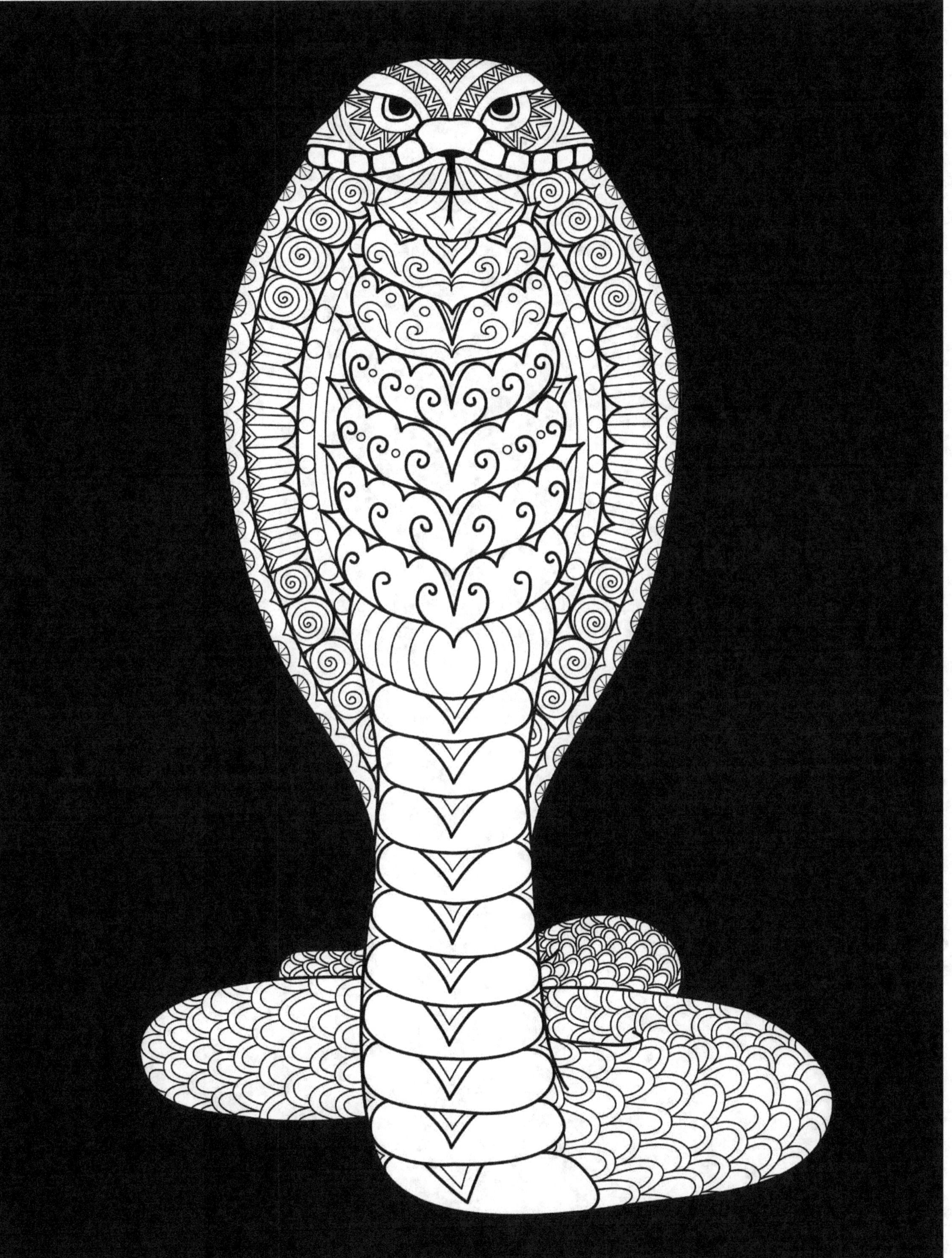

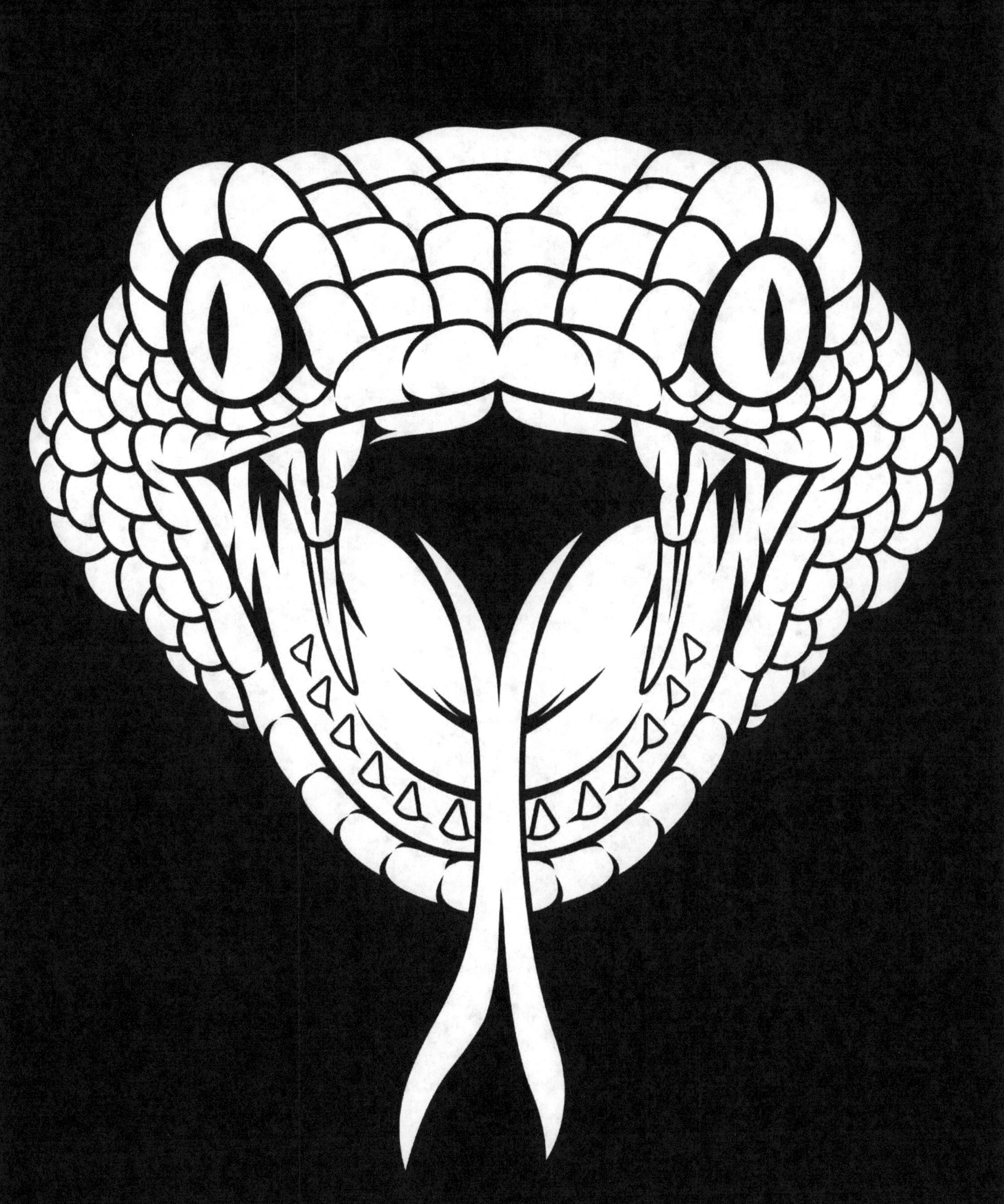

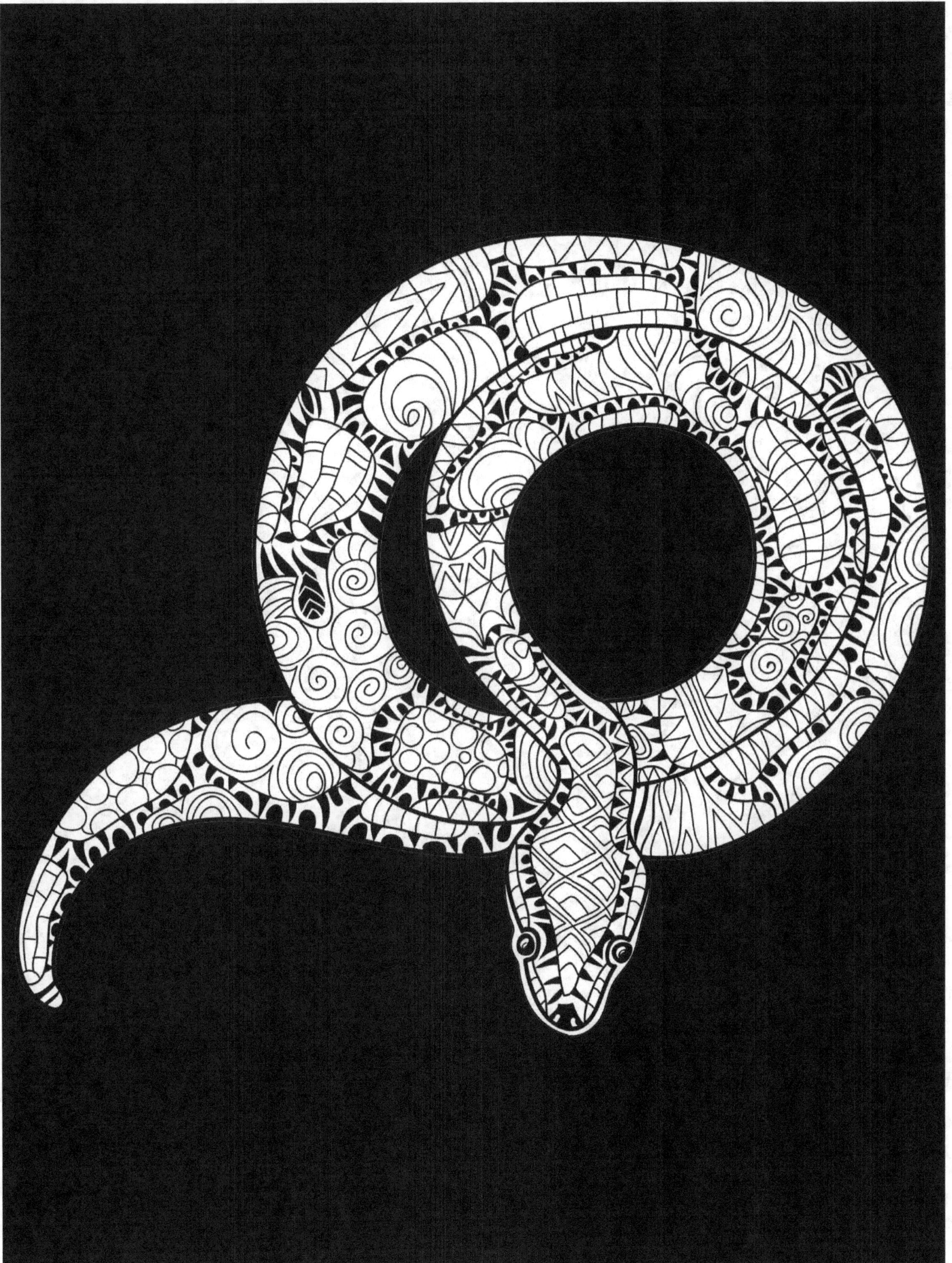

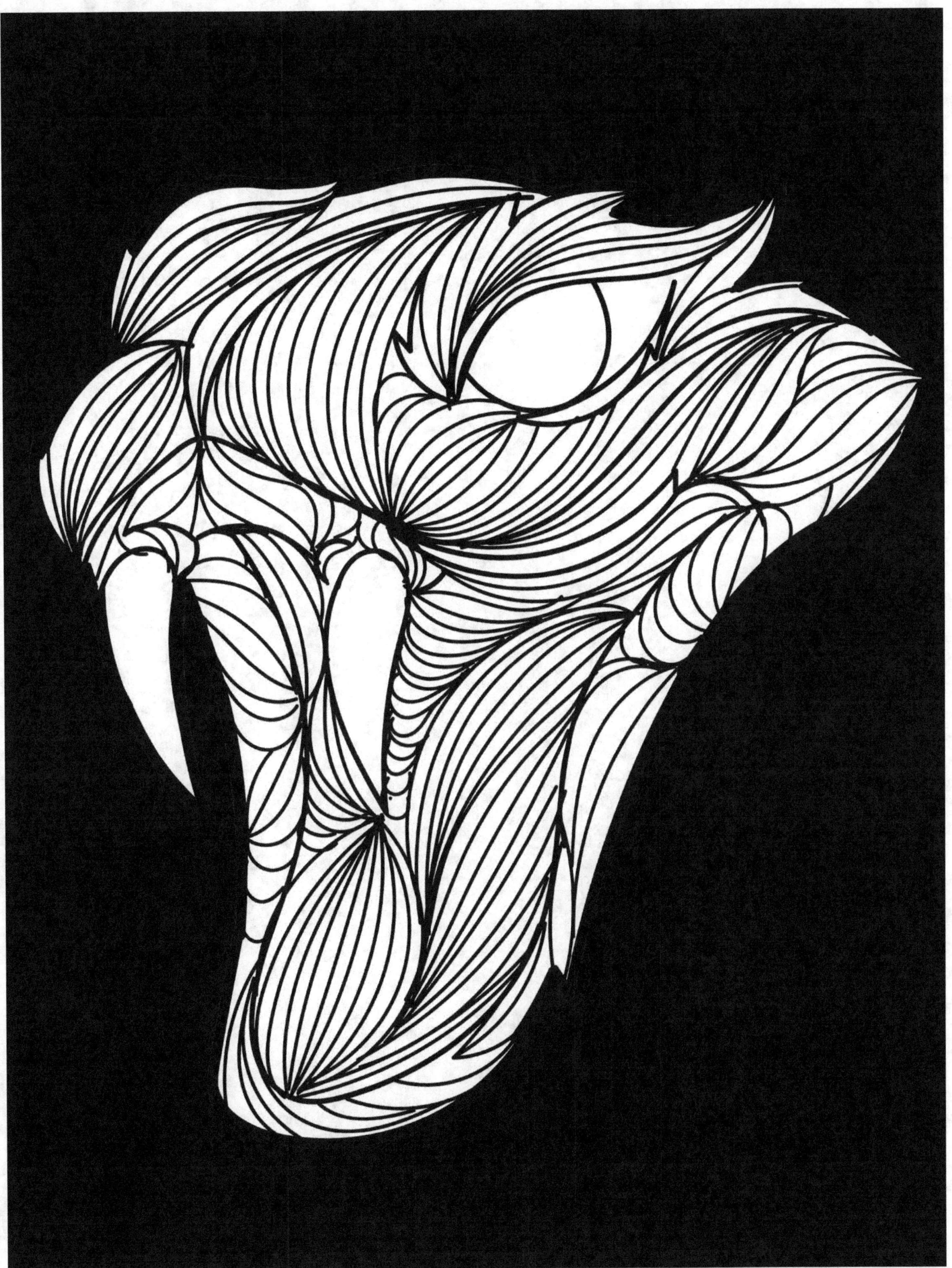

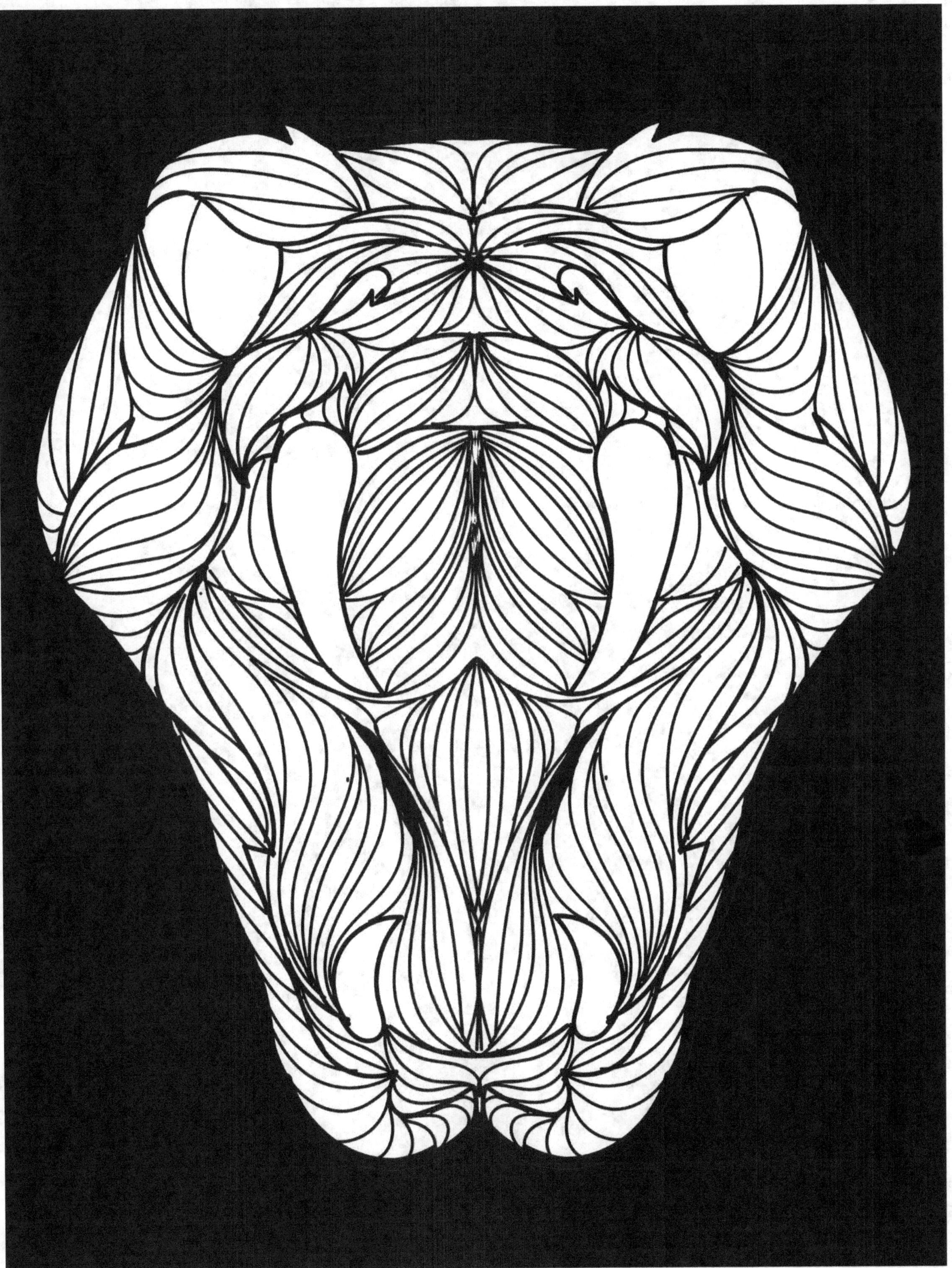

Check out more of our adult coloring and activity books!
Skull Crafts Publications
KILLER CLOWN
ADULT COLORING BOOK
PSYCHEDELIC COLORING BOOK
FACE MASK
Quarantine Coloring
WOLVES
ADULT COLORING BOOK